54 ways to get merchandise for your EBay Business

Proven Websites and Places to Get Products Cheap For EBay Success

Table of Contents

Cardinal Rules for Sourcing EBay Products

The first rule is to know the sale price before you buy the merchandise. You should never blindly buy merchandise if you have no idea what you will probably be able to sell it for no matter how cheap the merchandise is. You need to be able to do research on your potential product before you go about buying it. This is something I spend most of my time doing because I don't want to be stuck with merchandise that I can't sell and sell for a decent profit. An okay way to do mediocre research on a product is to search for it on EBay, and then use the filters on the left-side that say "Completed listings" and look at the auctions that have green numbers because that means these items sold. Look at about 15 or 20 of these auctions and calculated an average price. Now if you could get insider information about how a product is selling on EBay and I mean information like the average price, what day to post your auction, what category to post it in, and how long to set your auction; wouldn't you find that information priceless? There is a service that I have been using for years and I pay about $30 per month for it but I have extra features, it is as cheap as $24.95 and if you are sourcing product you will need to know what the going price is for it on EBay. Go to the resources website for this book at www.merch4ebay.com/insiderinfo to get the insider EBay information.

Second rule is to think like your customer; what would your customer think if they received this merchandise? Is it packaged well, is it in good condition? EBay buyers are picky people and you don't want to upset them because they will give you negative feedback. If the merchandise is dirty from sitting in a warehouse or the sealed wrapping is all torn up you should look elsewhere because you can't sell that as brand new.

Third rule is not to fully commit just to one product or wholesale supplier. I have seen wholesalers go out of business all the time so you must have a diversified supply chain of goods. Shopping around is always good you might find your product cheaper and shipped faster with another supplier. Now with merchandise let's say you want to sell IPods. You have to realize that sourcing IPods are almost impossible and that when you do find them you probably have to shell out over six thousand dollars. There are probably millions of different items people are buying on EBay so don't settle on selling just one thing, diversity is the key to this rule.

Last rule is to have fun and don't let these wholesalers get you upset. You will encounter some anal retentive people who are looking for thousand dollar orders and don't care about you. Don't let them upset you and remember there are thousands of wholesalers out there and they just lost a good customer. EBay is supposed to be fun and profitable, don't forget the fun part.

Resources Website

Make sure that you check out the resources website which is only for you the buyer of this book. You will get the links to the content referenced in this book and you will also get information on more wholesale sources as well as EBay

resources and some free stuff too. The resources website to

this book is www.merch4ebay.com

#1 Garage Sale

Garage Sales are perfect places to get items at very cheap

prices. Silverware, jewelry, plates, old children toys and things

of that nature are perfect things to pickup at a garage sale.

Don't be scared to price haggle for cheaper prices. Your

newspaper and local flyer list upcoming garage sales.

#2 Craigslist.com

This is an awesome place to get all kinds of merchandise to sell on EBay. People are selling everything here from jewelry to cars and all you have to do is call them, negotiate a price, and schedule a time for pickup and payment. I would always recommend that you have a person with you when you meet up to make an exchange. Your life and body is not worth getting beat up over some junk so always meet in a public place and have someone with you.

#3 Goodwill Thrift Store

The Goodwill thrift store is an awesome place to find things to sell on EBay, the price are low and many times you can find brand new designer clothing there in the store. When a department store doesn't sell its merchandise and it doesn't go to a closeout center, they just give it away to charity. Also go to a Goodwill store in a nice neighborhood, you will most of the time find nicer things.

#4 Goodwill Website

This website is one of the internet's best kept secrets. There are amazing things for sale on this website; I have seen boxes upon boxes of baseball cards, old comic books, new sealed video games, coins, and vintage guitars. Not a lot of people know about this website so don't let the secret out you paid for this book and this source alone is worth the cost of this book. Oh you can also find autographed pictures of athletes and Celebrities here also. Website: www.shopgoodwill.com

#5 Estate Auctions

Estate auctions maybe bad for the one holding the auction but it is good for you. You will find jewelry, cars, clothes, electronics and more. Look in your local newspaper or local business journals to find these types of auctions because by law these auctions need to be published in some sort of publication. Ask an attorney where most of these auctions are normally published.

#6 Local Government Surplus Store

Your local county or city government sells their old computers, vehicles, fax machines, furniture and more. The items usually are sold at a storage facility, an auction, or even a website. Contact your local government for information on where to purchase surplus items.

#7 Ebay.com, EBay UK, EBay Canada

This is a very cool concept that has been done mostly with cell phones. You go on EBay UK or Canada and purchase an item and then sell on the EBay U.S. site. The reason why this works real well for cell phones is because cell phones come out in the U.K. before the United States so by the time it's new in the U.S.; it's old in the U.K. meaning the price of it will be a lot lower. So you buy the phone for cheap in the U.K. and sell high in the U.S. There is a book out for sale about this cell phone method, if you want more details go to the resources website. Website: www.merch4ebay.com

#8 Storage Auction

This is a great source for all kinds' items to sell. When a person
doesn't pay their rent on their storage unit they get evicted.
The storage company auctions off the contents of the storage
unit to recoup the lost rent that wasn't paid for the many
months. You find a lot of Swap Meet sellers at these auctions.
Again these type of auctions need to be published so you can
find listing of them in the newspaper or local business journal or
even better go to a storage place and ask when there is going to
be an auction coming up.

#9 Kijiji

This is a classified website that actually was created by EBay.

You can find items for sale here and the sellers a lot of times

want to be paid online. Website: www.Kijiji.com

#10 Backpage

This is another classified ad website where you can find items

very cheap. Don't be afraid to look at other locations besides

the one that you live in. Website: www.backpage.com

#11 Free Cycle

This website is where a person can join a local community and post items that you are giving away for free. You don't have to pay a dime for these items you just go and pick it up. Website: www.freecycle.org

#12 Neiman Marcus Outlet

The store is called Neiman Marcus Last Call and you can find awesome prices on designer clothing. You find racks upon racks of discounted clothing that has colored tags that signify the amount of discount available. You can find Last Call stores all over the nation search "neiman marcus last call" to get locations.

#13 DH Gate

This is one of my favorite sources. The website is www.dhgate.com and you can find thousands of items of merchandise for sale that come directly from China. When you purchase items your money is held in escrow so if you are un-happy with the merchandise you just file a dispute and you get your money back. You can pay by credit card, PayPal and more. You can find incredible prices for electronics, clothing, and so much more. The sellers are ranked on a feedback system very similar to EBay with positive and negative feedbacks. I recommend you purchase from sellers with a feedback over 96% and make sure that their transaction number is over 100.

Website: www.dhgate.com

#14 Wholesale Central Network

The website is www.wholesalecentral.com; this website has hundreds of wholesale websites and sellers that sell too many things to list. There is a search box on the site so you can find what you're looking for. Understand that wholesale companies pay wholesale central to include their website in the directory and searches so there are many different businesses here and this source alone could have you in business up and running.

Website: www.wholesalecentral.com

#15 Wholesale Central Asia

This website is a spin-off associated with wholesale central. The buyers here are from china and they have a lot of more current merchandise at low prices. I would recommend trying DH Gate first before trying this website. Website:

www.wholesalecentral.com/Asian_Sources.html

#16 Closeout Central Network

Another website associated with wholesale central. This website has random items in categories at break neck prices. It is always good to check this site on a weekly basis. Website:

www.closeoutcentral.com

#17 Wholesale Gopher

Wholesale Gopher is similar to wholesale central and you might see some of the same wholesalers advertising on this site but you will find new ones here also that are not on wholesale central. Website: www.wholesalegopher.com

#18 Sumner Communications

Sumner is a company that publishes directories of wholesale

companies and other information. The books are very thick and

not very expensive. Website: www.sumnercom.com

#19 The Closeout News and Wholesale Merchandise Magazines

These are two excellent magazines filled with opportunity to

purchase goods for sale at very low prices. Subscription is not

cheap but well worth it. Website: www.thecloseoutnews.com

#20 Wholesale Source Magazine

This is a new magazine that post different types of wholesalers.

The subscription is not very expensive. Website:

www.Wsmag.com

#21 Your Own Home

This is one of the most obvious places to look but the most overlooked. You will be surprised what you have in your home just laying around in your garage, attic, basement, or home office.

#22 Unclaimed Packages

The U.S. Postal Service has an auction that occurs once a month

in Atlanta, GA if you go to their website

www.usps.com/auctions you will find a listing of their auction

dates. These are unclaimed and undelivered packages.

#23 UPS/FedEx Undelivered Packages

UPS and FedEx both use this company to sell of undelivered
packages. This company is in Utah and they have auctions
weekly. This company is planning to have online auctions but as
of this writing it hasn't happened yet. The website:

www.bukoos.com

#24 The Airport

Many airports accumulate large amounts of unclaimed baggage
and packages. These bags contain more than just stinky gym
socks you can find laptops, gifts, jewelry, and designer clothing.
My major airport is so large and has so much traffic that it holds
an auction once a year. Call your local airport to find out the
next auction.

#25 Federal Government Surplus.

The federal government sells equipment, electronics, and automobiles on their surplus website got to usa.gov and search for surplus items there. Website: www.usa.gov

#26 Customs and U.S. Marshalls Auction

Customs and the U.S. Marshalls auction off merchandise

confiscated by criminals and businesses all the time at various

locations nationwide search for Treasury Auctions to find this

information on federal government website. Website:

www.usa.gov

#27 IRS Auction

The IRS also auctions off land, homes, and merchandise search for treasury auctions also to find out what they have and where to bid for it.

#28 Liquidity Services

Liquidation.com is where companies like retail stores sell bulk amounts of overstocked merchandise, merchandise returns, and other conditions of merchandise. You must be prepared to buy in large quantities like 3,000 naval rings or 100 brand new laptops. You can make great margins selling these items on EBay. Website: www.liquidation.com

#29 Liquidity Services Government

Gov Liquidation offers items for sale from many different govemment departments like the army, the navy, the justice department etc...you can find both domestic and industrial items here. Website: www.govliquidation.com

#30 Go Wholesale Network

Gowholesale.com is another search engine of wholesale

companies; again you will see some similar results from

previous wholesale search engines buy you will also find new

ones. Website: www.Gowholesale.com

#31 Importers Network

Importers.com is a huge website directory of over 200,000

international companies and internet resources that make it

easy to buy merchandise from this site. Website:

www.Importers.com

#32 Alibaba

Alibaba is another website that has listings of thousands upon thousands of items that can be shipped from China. You have to be very careful with this website though because your money is not held in escrow and for the most case you have to send money to the supplier via Western Union. Look for gold suppliers only. Website: www.alibaba.com

#33 Charities / Charity Auctions

Charities are always looking for ways to raise money. So

approach any number of charities and offer to auction of items

that they can collect from important people and corporations

and you auction the items off for them and take a percentage of

the sale.

#34 Consignment for Others

Consignment is a very good way to get started in EBay. You will find people who have things lying around the house and want to sell them but they have no time to do it. So you negotiate a percentage of the sale to go to you and you put the item on EBay yourself. There is an awesome book about consignment on EBay that I have purchased and read go to resources website for this book to get the information. Website:

www.merch4ebay.com/consignmentbook

#35 Local Flyer / Newspaper Classifieds

People are always trying to sell their items on the local classified

ads and a lot of times you can get great prices on electronics

and media. Remember to always negotiate a price never take

the asking price as the final price.

#36 Copart

Copart is a major network of facilities that have automobiles that have been bank repossessed, submitted from insurance companies, and tow companies. A lot of the vehicles have clean titles, re-buildable titles, and vehicles for parts. A lot of the vehicles are available to the public and most require some sort of used car dealer to get the car for you. There are links on the website to get you linked up with a dealer to get a vehicle for you. No matter where the car is in the U.S. it can be shipped to you. You can purchase vehicles that have no damage, starts and drives, and has no problems for 90% less of what the car is worth. Website: www.copart.com

#37 Police Auctions

Police auctions consist of many things like vehicles, jewelry, electronics and everything else. You just have to know where the auction information is published so that you can visit and bid on items. Go to your local police department to get that information.

#38 Property Room

This is a website that many police agencies across the country use to auction off some of their confiscated items. You will find all kinds of great goodies here. Website:

www.propertyroom.com

#39 Overstock.com Auctions

This is a website not many people know about. This site is really an EBay copy with feedback and stuff like that. Since many people don't know about the site, you can get great deals on stuff and turn around and sell it on EBay. Go to overstock.com and look for auctions. Website: www.overstock.com

#40 Half.com

Half.com is an EBay Website and it specializes in textbooks,

music, movies, and other forms of Media. Many people use this

site but not as much as EBay. This means that you can purchase

a movie or video game cheaper at Half.com and re-sell it on

EBay for a higher amount. Website: www.half.com

#41 Local businesses

If you approach a local business and offer to get rid of non-

performing inventory they will be all ears. Yes they could sell

the stuff on EBay themselves but many don't have the time or

patience, and they won't have the amount of positive f eedback

as a seller as you do.

#42 Real Estate Agents

Real estate agents are highly motivated individuals who want to get their properties sold. Real estate agents not only have homes to sell but also vacant land. If you approach a real estate agent and tell them that you can sell their vacant lot or property in a week they will take you up on that offer. I would recommend trying this on vacant land first before trying a home or condo.

#43 Bid For Assets

Another great site used by many municipalities across the

United States. You will find vehicles, vacant land, houses,

paintings and more. The U.S. Marshalls have an online

agreement with this website to sell some its merchandise. Also

you can purchase tax deeds of properties which you can sell on

EBay or keep them.

#44 Flea Markets and Swap Meets

This is a type of bazaar where inexpensive or even secondhand goods are sold or bartered. There can be flea markets in or out doors. The vendors range from a family getting rid of unwanted goods to a commercial business that sells all sorts of goods that it has gotten from garage sales and storage auctions. Do a Google search for flea markets or swap meets and put in your location. Also Sumner Communications idea #18 sells a flea market directory.

#45 Dropshipping

Dropshipping basically is when you sell items that you don't physically have in your possession. When you make a sell you pay another company for the product and they in turn ship the product to the person you sold the merchandise too. You keep the difference of what you sold the item for minus the amount the merchandise cost. Dropshipping is a great way to start an EBay business without having the risk of committing to inventory. One of the cons to Dropshipping is you probably will see less profit for an item as oppose to if you purchased it in bulk. Many of the sources in this book offer Dropshipping, you will have to inquire about it.

#46 Going out of Business Sales / Auctions

This is another type of auction that will be published in your local news papers and business journals. When restaurants or other types of businesses go out of business, the bank or its lenders have the contents and inventory of the business auctioned off. You can get very good deals on inventory here.

#47 Contact Manufacturer

You will be surprised to find out how much you can get

accomplished by calling the manufacturer of a product. You will

get the names and phone numbers of local distributors as well

as requirements for becoming a reseller. If they want to know

how you do business always so you have an online store.

#48 Tow Service Auction

This is another published auction and is very similar to the

storage auctions. A car gets towed and the owner never

redeems their car back. So the Tower Company auctions off the

car for storage space that the car has used. You will be

surprised how many cars get auction off like this in a big city.

#49 World Wide Brands

This company is one of the only companies that EBay approves as a source for getting merchandise to sell for EBay. The Beauty of this company is that they have contacted thousands of wholesale suppliers and negotiated with them to sell merchandise to EBay Sellers. Many of these sellers will even drop ship items for you. To get access to this service it will cost some money but if you go to the resources website there is a coupon for a discount.   Website:

www.merch4ebay.com/wwbrands

#50 Saks 5th Ave Outlet

Saks Fifth Avenue OFF 5th is the discount designer store for Saks Fifth Avenue. You will find designer clothing at remarkable discounts of 40% to 70%. There are 55 of these stores across the United States. www.saksincorporated.com has more information and store locations. Website:

www.sacksincorporated.com

#51 Premium Outlets

You have probably been to a Chelsea Premium Outlet and don't

realize it. Remember when you went to Disney World and on

the day you went shopping you went into that huge outlet that

had brands like Movado, Timberland, Tommy, Nike, Adidas

Etc...well that's what I'm talking about. These outlets are all

over the U.S. even in Hawaii. If you go to the clearance racks

you will find all kinds of awesome deals. Website:

www.premiumoutlets.com

#52 Local Library

Local libraries have book sales all of the time. You will find old books, Old vintage music records still in the sleeves, and much more. You won't be disappointed going to one of these sales. Contact your local library for future sale information.

#53 Ioffer.com

This is another marketplace type website where people are selling all kinds of merchandise. You will find that sellers have feedback and many don't. Ask as many questions as you have when you talk to a seller and be very careful giving out money.

Website: www.ioffer.com

#54 Trade Show

This is an excellent way to source product for sale. You will be able to see the actual product and many times even get a chance to purchase a couple of pieces of product to test on EBay. The Best part is that you will meet the seller face to face and you can build a great relationship with this person. This can lead to the vendor lessening their rules on minimum purchase amounts and letting you know what new items are hot and trendy among other things. Go to the website of the closest convention center to you and get their schedule of upcoming events.

www.ingramcontent.com/pod-product-compliance
Lightning Source LLC
Chambersburg PA
CBHW051244170526
45165CB00004B/1563